Living For Fun

Heather Adams

BookLeaf
Publishing

Presentation by *BookLeaf Publishing*

Web: www.bookleafpub.com

E-mail: info@bookleafpub.com

ISBN: 9789358368581

First edition 2023

RD2

Risking dishonor
Gunfire explodes on horseback
Train robbing is fun

Spring

Sun in the sky
Provides food for the plants
Rain flows in swollen streams
Irrigating the valleys
Nature
Gives thanks in flowers

Gg

I mourned you in life when you made me feel
bad. I mourn you in death because I don't feel
sad. I wish that your presence had been as
peaceful as your absence. Holidays are brighter
and the air in the room feels lighter. No one is
upset when we get together. But no one takes
pictures and they fix the beans wrong.
Nobody worries all day long.
And nobody worries all day long.
You are missed dearly when coffee is made or
watering plants, and when telling old stories
with the uncles and aunts.

The Trap

I have a neighbor named Dan,
who plotted for kids with a scam
he tried and he tried
and eventually cried
and now he drives a van.

Trust

My heart
now cold and hard
beats with effort for you
waiting for someone to warm it
with trust

Wild Turkey

Looking
I range my bird
pulling my bowstring tight
I release and stick my dinner
It's fowl.

Faker

I don't know why you wave
why you smile
why you stop to talk
everything is on your terms
I don't accept those terms
I'll keep my waves and my smiles
and save my talk for someone who listens

Learning Dreams

When I'm stressed out my dreams reflect that
someone is trying to hurt me
trying to kill me
maybe it's an animal or a person with no face
dreams are where it's safe to fail
but in dreams I never do
I always wake up first
Fat and I you know that

Alabama Cheesehound

The first dog I had who loved to scent roll
Happiest when the scent is death
Open to growing her pack
Raised my kids as her own and rescued a cat
Always kept my secrets

Beware The Treeguard

I hear doggies
run to the beefalo
but don't let the torch go out after dark

daisy chains and shaving face
can save your sanity
but nothing can save your berries
from the gobblers

tacocat

The executioner of leaves
Always making biscuits on the dog
Cannot sleep less than 23 hours a day
Openly mocks me when I sing his theme song

In The Pines

Beautiful pine
heavy with snowy branches
falling to the ground

SW

Seeing the good in a situation
Offering unconditional positive regard
Cleaning everything all of the time
Intuition keeps people alive
Always leave your location on
Let clients know about all available options

When to visit the jail
Overlooking being yelled at
Reframing situations for clients
Keeping goals prioritized
Encourage client's to use coping skills
Resources help meet basic needs

Working

I want to work to live
I don't want to live to work
I want to take vacations every season
I want to go places I've never been before
I don't want to work
more than is necessary
to pay bills

A Good Day

A good day
starts with coffee on the porch
sun on my face
music on the radio
a blank page in my journal
a good day ends with a job well done

Self-care

Throat hurts
ears full
I don't want to go
to work or school
the more I rest
the better I'll feel
never negotiate self-care
that cannot be part of the deal

SLEEP

Settling in for the night
Letting go of things
Examining the days events
Everything can wait until tomorrow
Phone is off

Grace

Give yourself the grace that you give to others.
If you met yourself on the street would you be
proud of your interaction?